Web Content Management For Dummies®

by Nathan Rawlins

WILEY

Wiley Publishing, Inc.

Web Content Management For Dummies®

Published by
Wiley Publishing, Inc.
111 River Street
Hoboken, NJ 07030-5774

Published by Wiley Publishing, Inc., Indianapolis, Indiana

Published simultaneously in Canada

For general information on our other products and services or to obtain technical support, please contact our Customer Care Department within the U.S. at 800-762-2974, outside the U.S. at 317-572-3993, or fax 317-572-4002.

Wiley also publishes its books in a variety of electronic formats. Some content that appears in print may not be available in electronic books.

ISBN: 0-7645-7928-2

Manufactured in the United States of America

10 9 8 7 6 5 4 3 2

1O/QT/QZ/QU/IN

WILEY

Publisher's Acknowledgments

We're proud of this book; please send us your comments through our online registration form located at www.dummies.com/register/.

Some of the people who helped bring this book to market include the following:

Acquisitions, Editorial, and Media Development

Development Editor: Clark Scheffy

Senior Project Editor: Zoë Wykes

Editorial Manager: Rev Mengle

Media Development Manager: Laura VanWinkle

Media Development Supervisor: Richard Graves

Cartoons: Rich Tennant, www.the5thwave.com

Composition

Project Coordinator: Kristie Rees

Layout and Graphics: Lauren Goddard, Michael Kruzil, Melanee Prendergast, Heather Ryan, Julie Trippetti

Proofreaders: Dwight Ramsey, Brian H. Walls

Indexer: Joan Griffitts

Special Help

From Wiley: Gabriele McCann

From Serena: Ed Rarick, Jeff Wheeler, Laura Cox, Maciej Chodzko-Zajko, Mitzi Sandman, September Danforth, Tim Zonca, Vickie Schira-Malde

---

Publishing and Editorial for Technology Dummies

Richard Swadley, Vice President and Executive Group Publisher

Andy Cummings, Vice President and Publisher

Mary Bednarek, Executive Acquisitions Director

Mary C. Corder, Editorial Director

Publishing for Consumer Dummies

Diane Graves Steele, Vice President and Publisher

Joyce Pepple, Acquisitions Director

Composition Services

Gerry Fahey, Vice President of Production Services

Debbie Stailey, Director of Composition Services

Table of Contents

Introduction

Chances are, if you're taking the time to read this book, you have a vested interest in some Web site out there on the vast World Wide Web. Perhaps you are a Webmaster. Or a marketing manager. Maybe you're simply a concerned corporate citizen who cares about the message you're sending your customers. Whatever your position, you have important Web sites that need to be managed better.

REMEMBER

For the sake of simplicity, I refer to the people you care to communicate with as your *customers,* meaning anyone who you want to see your Web content. These people may be your business prospects, employees, students, citizens of the great community you live in — *customers* in the broadest sense of the word.

The Web has completely changed the way you communicate with customers. Only a few years ago, communicating with customers was a tremendous task. Remember the days when you had to actually print and mail communications? Remember when your glossy marketing slick was the main way you had of presenting your image? Well, those days have gone the way of Cyndi Lauper. Sure, we still send out printed communications, and we probably still have a nice glossy marketing slick. (And some of us may admit to listening to Cyndi Lauper now and again, but that really isn't the point.) Your Web site has probably replaced mailed communications as your primary means for communicating with your customers.

No wonder then that you're concerned about the challenges of managing changes to your Web site. Rest assured, you're not alone. Most organizations on the planet are using inefficient means to manage Web content.

That's where this handy little book comes in. This book is designed to help you get started on the path to Web content management bliss. With some careful planning and a little work, you can make managing changes to Web content a lot easier, a lot more efficient, and a whole lot more effective.

I can't offer an exhaustive reference about all things Web-related in the space of this book. The goal is really to give you just enough to get you started. Just enough to help you understand why you have the problems you have, and where you can go for help. I'm confident that this book will enable you to identify challenges in your Web content management and ask the right questions to determine the appropriate solution.

Who Should Read This Book

If you care about your Web site, this book is for you. What your job title is or whether you work for a huge corporation or the planning board for a small province in France doesn't matter. The Web has made publishers of us all. No matter what your background, this book can help you understand the issues surrounding Web content management, the basic solutions for helping you manage that content, and where to go next to get more help.

How to Use This Book

Web Content Management For Dummies is organized so that you can cuddle up with a hot cup of tea and read it like a novel or just flip through it to find areas of particular interest. Whether you're completely new to managing Web content or an old pro, you'll be able to find information in this book to help make your Web site hum along like a well-oiled machine.

How This Book Is Organized

This book is organized into three main parts, each with a specific focus.

Part I: Introducing Content Management

You may be surprised to discover that if you have a Web site, you already have a content management system. The focus of this section is to help you determine whether you can improve that content management system. I explain in plain language the issues that can thwart efficient and effective content management. I also build up some basic understanding of how Web content works so that you have the tools to solve any content management problems.

Part II: Content Management Fundamentals

If you have a content management problem, a packaged content management system may be just what the doctor ordered. In this part, I discuss the different parts of a content management system and how those different parts can work together to make changing Web content a snap.

Part III: The Part of Tens

No *For Dummies* book is really a *For Dummies* book without the Part of Tens. In this section, I include a chapter with some best practices for ensuring that you get the most out of your Web content management system and a chapter with some Web basics as well.

Icons Used in This Book

As you may have already noticed, I use icons to point out bits and pieces of information with special importance:

Memorize this, be prepared to recite it as poetry or tattoo it to the soles of your feet. This is good stuff to keep in mind.

If anything I discuss gets a bit "back office," I let you know with this icon.

Twenty percent is not unheard of, but I'll be happy if you just take these bits as sound advice from an old pro.

The bomb with the lit fuse from this icon is a bit extreme — nothing in this book will explode, or even make you itch. The warning icon just alerts you to an issue requiring a bit of extra attention.

Assumptions and Other Important Stuff

I assume that you have at least a basic familiarity with the Web and how Web sites work. If you're unfamiliar with some of the basics, I include a handy 10,000-foot view of the Web in the Part of Tens.

Part I

Introducing Content Management

The 5th Wave By Rich Tennant

"Maybe it would help our Web site if we showed our products in action."

In this part . . .

Do you need some help to better manage changes to your Web content? In this part, I help you identify whether you have a Web content management problem and explain in part how you can solve it.

Chapter 1

Do You Even Need a Content Management System?

In This Chapter

- Understanding whether you have a content management problem
- Taking stock of your management needs
- Introducing content management systems

So, you think you may need a content management system. You may be surprised to discover that you already have one. If you have a Web site, you already have a content management system in place.

A *content management system* is simply some process for managing content on your Web site. Perhaps you paid money for software that helps manage that process. Maybe your current system was built by some in-house techno-wiz. Or, it could be that you manage your content by typing stuff in Word and sending it to a Web guru to put on the Web. Whatever you do, you have a system.

However, until you have a basic understanding of how your system works (or doesn't work), knowing how you can improve it is challenging.

A Quick Quiz

A pop quiz on the first day? Don't panic. This should be easy. To help you decide whether you need to make changes to your existing system, take a minute to answer "True" or "False" to the following statements:

1. Updating critical Web content takes too long.
2. Our IT staff is overwhelmed by requests to make changes to the Web site.
3. The people responsible for our Web content don't have access to make any changes.
4. Our Web site doesn't have consistent branding, look and feel, or navigation.
5. We don't have insight into who changed what and when.
6. We can publish our site only every week or so.

If you said "True" to any of these questions, you have yourself a true-blue content management challenge. The more often you said "True," the bigger that challenge is. That's the bad news. The good news is that there's help out there.

So, What's a CMS, Anyway?

A *CMS (Content Management System)* is a system that's designed to help you manage your Web content publishing process. Believe it or not, content management systems have been around for a long time. In fact, they've been around a lot longer than the Web.

A lot has changed in the last few years, however. Organizations already have Web sites in production use. Most of these Web sites were created with authoring tools like Macromedia Dreamweaver or Microsoft FrontPage, and may use one of several scripting languages like ASP, JSP, PHP, or ColdFusion to assemble and deliver the content. Today's content management problem is more about helping organizations manage these *existing* sites than helping Web development teams create new ones from scratch. This difference may be subtle, but it strongly affects the way you approach content management.

The evolution of content management

As you look for solutions to your content management problem, understanding a bit about the evolution of the content management industry may be helpful.

Long before the Web was wildly popular, large-scale publishers used systems for managing print production. As the Web caught on, it was only natural that companies with print production roots (such as newspapers) sought to take advantage of the new medium.

Many packaged content management systems were designed for the publishing industry (and in some cases by publishers themselves) and were adapted for the rest of us — the "accidental publishers," as we were called. Other systems started out as document repositories and later had Web capabilities bolted and duct-taped on top of them. All of these early systems had at least one thing in common: The systems were designed for organizations that were building *new* Web sites.

Chapter 2

What Is Content, Anyway?

In This Chapter

- Understanding what is, and what is not, content
- Distinguishing structured and unstructured content
- Deciphering metadata
- Separating form and content
- Sharing and reusing content

Before I blather on about managing Web content, it's probably a good idea to discuss what I mean by content.

Content can be many different things. Content may be a bunch of text in the form of an article. It may be a video clip. It could be a list of employee names. It could even be programming code. All of the following elements are examples of the type of content that makes up common Web pages:

- **Documents:** Microsoft Word docs, Adobe Acrobat docs (PDFs), and so on.
- **Text:** You know, a whole bunch of words.
- **Images:** On the Web, images are usually in the form of JPEGs or GIFs.
- **Rich media:** Macromedia Flash files, video, audio.
- **Code:** Web-based programs that add functions to your Web site in languages like ASP, ColdFusion, JavaScript, and so on.

Sometimes the word *content* is used to describe any building block of a Web site, including navigational components, style sheets, or even application code. We could debate all day whether these elements are technically content. But that's no fun, so I just sidestep the issue for now and call all of these things *assets*. The most important thing to recognize is that all assets can benefit from a little management!

Structured and Unstructured Content

Web content comes in two main flavors: structured and unstructured. These two types of content are managed in very different ways. As you figure out your strategy for managing your content better, understanding the distinction between the two types of content becomes important.

Structured content

Content is deemed *structured* when it includes some form or structure that defines the different parts of the content. For example, suppose you open Microsoft Word and write a press release. Chances are that you're going to follow some sort of pattern. You'll likely include a headline, perhaps an abstract summary, and then the body of the document. I know that you could easily identify these three distinct parts if you looked at one of my press releases. However, computers aren't so smart (unless you go to a lot of work to train them).

Just following a pattern doesn't necessarily make the content structured. A computer can't automatically tell the difference between a headline and a body unless you tell it which is which. In order to make your document structured (so that even a machine can figure it out), you need to add some information to the content that defines the structure of the document. Truly structured content includes an explicit designation of each element of the content. In the press release example, the elements are the headline, the summary, and the body.

You can accomplish the task of structuring content in several ways. Most content management systems use one or the other of the following (or a combination of both):

- **Databases:** Many content management systems actually store a piece of content chunked up into pieces. Each piece of the content is stored in a field in a database. An important press release from the USDA might look something like this when stored in a database:

Asset ID	***Headline***	***Abstract***	***Body***
13023212	Chocolate Key to Health	After extensive research, USDA scientists have discovered that five servings a day of chocolate will actually prevent all forms of disease and will not lead to obesity.	After more than ten years of double-blind, double chocolate fudge studies, the USDA is ready to announce revised guidance for dietary intake of chocolate...

- **XML:** XML is a markup language used to define the structure of a document. The press release would look something like this in XML:

```
<pressrelease>
<headline>Chocolate Key to Health</headline>
<abstract> After extensive research, USDA
scientists have discovered that five servings
a day of chocolate will actually prevent all
forms of disease and will not lead to
obesity.</abstract>
<body> After more than ten years of double-
blind, double chocolate fudge studies, the
USDA is ready to announce revised guidance
for dietary intake of chocolate . . . </body>
 </pressrelease>
```

Why should I care?

Structured content can be really handy. For example, say that you want to make a list of all the press releases on your site. Wouldn't it be great if some Web genius could write a bit of magic code that automatically makes a list of the headlines of the latest 10 press releases? Well, if your content is structured, that task is pretty simple. You or your awesomely tattooed Web dude just writes a piece of code that finds every `<headline>` tag and collects them all into a list. However, if your content isn't structured, it's likely going to take a bunch of manual work to make your list.

But isn't structuring content a real pain?

Yup, structuring content *can* be a real pain. But that's one of the many benefits of having a content management system. A good content management system makes it possible to create structured content without really knowing that you're creating structured content. The structuring process should be completely invisible to the people adding content to the Web site. After you have a content management system in place, adding structured content is relatively straightforward.

Depending on your needs, you may want to go back and add structure to your existing unstructured content. It's probably a good idea to do that incrementally. The most efficient course of action is to get basic control of your existing content first, and then visit the issue of whether to change the format of your legacy (older) content.

Unstructured content

Chances are most of your existing Web site content is *unstructured*. It's likely a bunch of pages that aren't broken down into classified elements, which is just fine. Not all content needs to be structured to be useful. As you discover how a content management system works, hopefully you'll start to see which content should be transitioned into structured content types and which make sense to leave unstructured.

A good content management system won't force you to transform all your existing unstructured content into structured content right away. A good system will allow you to make incremental changes to structure over time, as your needs change.

Structured Content Types

Various types of structured content follow different structures. Before you can begin creating structured content, you need to think about the different types of content you plan to manage. Think back to the press release example. The press release has three discrete parts:

- Headline
- Abstract
- Body

A job posting wouldn't follow the same structure. Perhaps a job posting would be broken down into:

- Job title
- Hiring department
- Job description
- Contact information

TIP

Before you begin the process of structuring content, sit down and define the different types of content you're going to manage. In this task, as in most content management tasks, erring on the side of simplicity is probably a good idea.

Metadata: Data about Data

If the term *metadata* conjures up bad memories of boring, completely ineffable college lectures, you're not alone. Even the conventional definition of metadata is completely confusing: *metadata is data about data*. Yeah, that helps.

So let's just skip the definition entirely and go straight to an example. Take the example of an image. An image is a piece of data. It's usually a file named something like dog.gif or dog.jpg. To make the image more useful, you may further define the image with some additional data, such as the following:

- Dimensions
- File size
- Creation date
- Keywords
- Description

And so on. All of these additional pieces of data are *metadata* — data that further describes another piece of data.

For good measure, go back to the press release example again. The press release broke down into three parts: headline, abstract, and body. The press release could have additional metadata to further define it, such as:

- Publication date
- Creation date
- Expiration date
- Last edited by

And so on.

Why metadata matters

Metadata is very important to effectively manage content. Here are just a few of the benefits of good metadata:

- **Metadata makes content more findable.** Instead of just searching on the name of an image, for example, you can search on keywords and other properties.
- **Metadata gives your content more "intelligence."** Good metadata can be used to tailor content to specific site visitors (also called personalization).
- **Metadata can be used to track important events, such as who last edited content, when content was last published, and so on.**

You can use all of this information to make your Web content more dynamic and more useful to you and your customers.

Separating Form and Content

If content management were a religion, the separation of form and content would be a key tenet. In practice, this means that the *form* (how the content looks, or is formatted) should be separate from the actual content itself.

Traditional publishers figured out long ago that by keeping form and content separate, they could more rapidly adapt to changing print formats. The same principles apply to the Web, sometimes for different reasons. Here are just a few reasons why keeping form and content separate is a good idea:

- **When you need to make a change, you can make the change once and have it universally applied.** For example, you may have a legal disclaimer that you include at the bottom of all your pages. The great thing about a content management system is that you can make a change to the disclaimer once, and every page that uses that disclaimer can be updated. Sure beats fixing issues page, by page, by page. . . .
- **Adding form to content is tedious and requires special skills.** Why trouble people with the details of HTML unless you absolutely have to?
- **Not everyone should be a designer.** The way you present your content says a lot about your organization. By keeping form separate from the content itself, you can pick and choose a qualified Web designer to muddle with the design of your site.
- **If form and content are separate, different formats can be applied to the same content, making it reusable.** For example, a piece of content could be published to your Web site, to a partner's site (with a completely different look and feel), and made available to be syndicated in structured XML for use on other Web sites.
- **If form and content are separate, reusing content is easier.** This point is so important that it deserves its own section, which comes up next.

Don't get caught up in the strict separation of form and content. Sometimes mixing the two is unavoidable. The important thing is to give form and content some thought to make sure that you aren't limiting your possibilities or causing yourself more work.

Sharing and Reusing Content

By sharing and reusing content, you can save yourself a lot of time, all the while making your content more valuable.

For content to be effectively reused, it needs to be structured and should maintain separation of content and form.

I want to go back to our old standby press release as an example. The whole point of a press release is to publicize something, and you'll likely try to get the press release posted in as many places as you can in order to increase the likelihood someone will read it. You may make the press release available in the following ways:

- On your public Internet site
- On your intranet site
- On a partner site
- On a wireless device (like a cellphone or a PDA)
- For syndication to other sites

Each of these destinations may require very different formatting to match the look and feel of the destination Web site, or even the display device in the case of content directed at a wireless device. Separating the form from the content makes applying a different format for different destinations programmatically easy to do.

The same principle applies when you use chunks (that is, structured pieces) of content in different places. On your site, you may have a list of the latest press releases. If your content is structured, writing a little script that will create a list of the latest press releases is pretty straightforward for a Web guru. The script would simply go through the store of press releases, pull out the headline of each press release, and display the resulting list. You may want the headlines to show up in the list as underlined hyperlinks, but as bold text on the release itself — unless the form and content are separate, that could be a painful (and time-consuming) task.

Content reuse goes far beyond simply deploying a piece of content to different destinations. Think about all the images on your site. Wouldn't it be great if you could use a single image across dozens of pages on your site and have the insight to know which pages would be impacted if you were to change the image? Wouldn't it be great if you could change the footer or legal notice once and have it automatically change across all the pages that use it? That's the beauty of reusing structured content.

Chapter 3

Choosing among CMS Architectures

In This Chapter

- Understanding how various content management systems work
- Dissecting the basic Web infrastructure into its component parts
- Picking the best CMS architecture for your needs

Before talking about the various CMS architectures, dissecting the basic anatomy of a typical Web infrastructure is probably a good idea.

Every system will have its quirks, but the components break out as follows:

- **Authoring environment:** Here you *author* (create) content. You can do so in Microsoft Word, Macromedia Dreamweaver, a home-grown CMS, and so on.
- **Staging Server:** Prior to publishing the content to the live site, you usually store the content on a staging server where the site can be tested. This system is usually inside the *firewall* (not accessible by the public). Once content is checked out on the staging server, you can send it to the "live" site on a delivery server, usually via FTP or some other standard Web protocol.
- **Delivery Server:** The delivery server is the machine that actually sends content to site visitors when they request it. The delivery server is outside the firewall in the case of a public site and likely inside the firewall for an intranet. The delivery server will have some sort of software to handle the requests for content and the delivery of the

content to the site visitor's client computer. This software may be a Web server (such as Apache, Microsoft IIS, or Netscape Web Server), an application server (such as BEA WebLogic, IBM WebSphere, or Apache Tomcat), and a portal server or a personalization server. Some early content management systems even performed the task of delivering content. The point is that you can perform the actual delivery of the content in many different ways.

TIP

Restricting content authors from making changes directly to the live Web site is a good idea. With a content management system, authors can make changes, preview what the changes will look like, and then publish them to the live server only when it's clear that the changes have been correctly made.

Different CMS Architectures

CMS architectures fall into two broad categories: *runtime* and *design-deploy*. Each category has advantages and disadvantages. In the next two sections, I talk briefly about each one.

Runtime

In the case of a *runtime* system, the content management system software runs in your authoring environment, your staging environment, and your delivery environment. The CMS actually performs the final delivery of the content to the site visitor.

Most runtime content management systems were designed in the days before good alternatives for delivering content existed. In lieu of good specific solutions for delivering the content, the CMS took on that job as well.

For organizations dealing with highly dynamic, large-scale Web sites (like an e-commerce site or a news site that gets millions of hits a day), the integrated runtime system may very well be the way to go.

WARNING!

Why don't all sites use runtime systems? Runtime systems generally introduce significant cost (you have to license the software for each server) and a bunch of complexity — after all, they were designed for hugely complex publishing challenges.

Design-deploy

A *design-deploy* system focuses on the management of the content and leaves the delivery of the content to another system. In other words, you use the CMS to create and manage the content and then publish the prepared content to the delivery server where some other software, Web server, application server, or portal server actually delivers the content to site visitors.

If you have a Web site, you already have some sort of software in place that does the job of delivering the content. A design-deploy system simply plugs into your existing infrastructure. Your delivery is performed by the system you already use, but you add the advantage of content management from your new design-deploy CMS. This can save you a whole lot of money and dramatically cut down on the system complexity.

So, what are the downsides of a design-deploy architecture? For the vast majority of organizations, a design-deploy architecture makes sense. A design-deploy system is a lot simpler and a whole lot less expensive than a runtime system. If you're looking to manage a highly dynamic site such as an e-commerce site, then perhaps going to a more complex runtime system is merited. Otherwise, your best bet is probably the simplicity of design-deploy.

Part II

Content Management Fundamentals

The 5th Wave By Rich Tennant

"You know, I've asked you a dozen times not to animate the torches on our Web page!"

In this part . . .

Most content management systems do a whole bunch of things — from helping you author new content, to managing the details of editing and collaborating on content, to actually publishing content. In this section, I focus on many of the different features you can expect to find in a good content management system.

Chapter 4

Getting Control of Your Existing Content

In This Chapter

- Importing content
- Making sense of content relationships
- Authoring new content
- Converting content

Does your content remind you of an unruly teenager: hard to deal with, seems to have a mind of its own, and never seems to be where it's supposed to be? If so, it's time to rein in that content, get it under control, and teach it a little discipline.

Actually, this process is a tad easier than parenting a teenager. With the right approach and the right tools, getting control of your existing content can be fast and fairly painless.

TIP

To take advantage of all the benefits a content management system has to offer, you need to structure some or all of your content, which I talk about in the next section. But that doesn't mean you can't get *any* benefit until you structure your content. In fact, you can get tremendous benefit from your CMS long before you start structuring content. Look for a CMS that lets you gain control fast, and then deal with structuring your content when you want to.

Reining In Your Content

You can get your existing content into a CMS in several ways. So, how do you decide which approach is best for you? It really depends on two things:

1. The capabilities of your CMS, and
2. The state of your existing content

The following sections provide some detail on the different approaches.

Gruntwork

This option is the least appealing of all the options, as the name implies. Unless your CMS doesn't support *import* (unfortunately quite a few don't), you shouldn't have to consider this option. The *gruntwork* method is just what it sounds like, which is basically a loooong exercise in copy and paste. Avoid this method if at all possible. It's about as fun as getting a root canal, or cleaning sewers. It is, however, a bit better than getting a root canal while cleaning sewers.

Dumb import

Dumb import is a step up from pure gruntwork, but it's still going to involve some work of the grunty variety. A *dumb import* sucks your existing content into the content repository and makes it available for management.

What dumb import *doesn't* do is much more important than what it does do. A dumb import doesn't have the intelligence to understand content relationships — that's why it's "dumb."

This calls for an example. Imagine for a moment that you are the esteemed Webmaster of a leading Jennifer Lopez fan site. This site is complex and changes frequently — especially that "People in J Lo's Life" page. The "People in J Lo's Life" page is called `people.html` and has links to all sorts of pages, including one about her latest guy-friend. Now, bear with me. This week, it's all about Ben Affleck and is called `ben-affleck.html`. In the case of a dumb import, when you import these pages, the link on `people.html` still points at the *other page* called `ben-affleck.html`. What's the problem with that, you say? Isn't that just what you want? Sorry to break it to you, but that isn't really what you want. Here's why.

In about the same time it takes you to import your site, our good friend Jennifer has gone off and found herself a new beau. So, you go in and update the Ben Affleck page with the skinny on the latest guy (I'd say it was Marc Anthony, but by the time you read this, there's a good chance I'd be wrong). Sensing a pattern, you decide to rename the page `latestguy.html` instead of using the latest guy's name. Good idea, but there's a problem. You now have yourself a broken link. You see, `people.html` still thinks it should look for `ben-affleck.html`, not `latestguy.html`. It's not smart enough to recognize that the page was renamed. So, how do you fix that?

Well, that's just one of the things a *smart import* CMS can do for you.

Smart import

Smart import does more than just import the content — smart import actually understands the relationships of the content it imports.

With a smart import, when the import comes across the link from `people.html` to `ben-affleck.html`, it says, "Hmm, looks like there's a relationship here; I really should keep track of this in case something changes." A smart import stores the details of the relationship and tracks any changes to the relationship, so that when something changes (like the page name), the software can automatically update the relationship. Handy, no? Figure 4-1 shows an example of a smart import screen.

But wait, there's more. A smart import can actually understand the dynamic elements of a page, such as content that is included at runtime by the delivery server, and treat them accordingly. Sometimes it takes training the software a little, but it's a heck of a lot better than weeks of gruntwork.

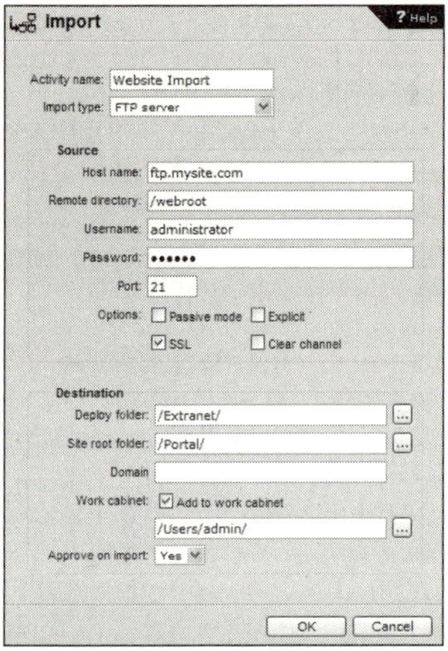

Figure 4-1: A sample smart import screen.

A smart import stores the content and relationships from your site so that if you want to, you can publish everything right back out to your delivery servers. It would look and function exactly as it did before — but would be a lot more intelligent and would recognize changes and relationships among the pages in your site.

What Import Buys You

You may not be able to get *all* the benefits of your CMS by just importing your content, but you can get a whole lot of benefit. In fact, I've come across many companies that decide that the benefits derived from getting control of their existing content is all they really need. Here are just a few of the benefits of getting basic control of your content (I talk about these benefits in more detail later):

- **Content versioning.** Every time you make a change to your content, the system stores a new version of the content so that you can keep track of changes and revert to previous versions if you need to.
- **Audit trails.** You can see who changed what and when.

- **Link validation.** You can make sure that all your links are healthy and happy.
- **Asset management.** You can manage different types of assets, such as images or Word documents, in ways that best suit the particular type of content.
- **Desktop integration.** That is, the ability to add content to the site from common desktop tools.
- **Workflow.** Manage the process of changing content on your site.
- **Managed publishing.** Managed publishing buys you a lot of things such as scheduled publishing, incremental publishing, and publishing reports — I talk about all of these in detail later.

Authoring New Content

Are you looking at a content management system to make it easier for many different people to add content to your Web site? If so, the authoring tools a CMS offers are probably of interest.

Sometimes the *authoring* capabilities of a content management system are referred to as *contribution* capabilities.

Many people don't like to learn new things — especially new software packages. So unless you want a mutiny on your hands, make sure to pay attention to how people will have to author content in your new CMS. The more it's like what they already know, the easier it's going to be to get people to use the system. Here are a few common ways of authoring Web content.

Desktop applications

Microsoft Word is one of the most common applications for creating content. It isn't a perfect application for creating Web content, but under the right circumstances, Word can work just fine. On the upside, just about everyone knows how to use Word. On the downside, historically Word hasn't done a very good job of adding structure to content. But that's starting to change. As Word matures, it will likely evolve into a much more viable application for creating structured Web content.

If you aren't very concerned about creating structured content, using Word may be the way to go because people are familiar with it. Just make sure that your CMS has an interface that makes it possible to save content directly to Word. The fewer steps a user has to take, the better.

HTML editors

Macromedia Dreamweaver and other HTML editors have a lot of the same benefits and downsides as Microsoft Word. While they are easy to use, they don't do a particularly good job of structuring content for content reuse. Further, they usually give the user a lot of control over look and feel, something that can be problematic if you're concerned about maintaining consistency among Web pages created by multiple authors.

Contribution

Contribution is a Web management term that basically means an authoring environment specifically created for easy authoring of structured Web content. Contribution systems vary from system to system, but generally fall into three broad categories:

- Forms-based contribution
- In-context contribution
- Drag-and-drop

The following three sections discuss these categories in more detail.

Forms-based contribution

With *forms-based contribution,* a form that a user can fill in to create new content is presented. Imagine a Web form with a form field for the header of a press release, another for the abstract, the body, and so on.

Some forms-based systems include a formatting toolbar as part of the form so that authors can make minor changes to the content formatting. Content management purists tend to really like forms-based interfaces, while casual users tend to despise forms-based interfaces for the same basic reason: Authoring content in a form gives you minimal control over formatting and little, if any, concept of how the content will ultimately look when it's viewed by a site visitor.

WARNING!

To see how the page will look, you have to preview it. Doing so isn't a big hassle, but it does tend to turn some people off.

In-context contribution

In-context contribution is a bit of a compromise between content management purists and casual users. When using in-context contribution, the user still fills out a form to add content, but the form is presented within the context of the active site. This is where a picture is worth a thousand words. Figure 4-2 shows a form for filling out a press release. Notice that the authoring environment looks just like an active page.

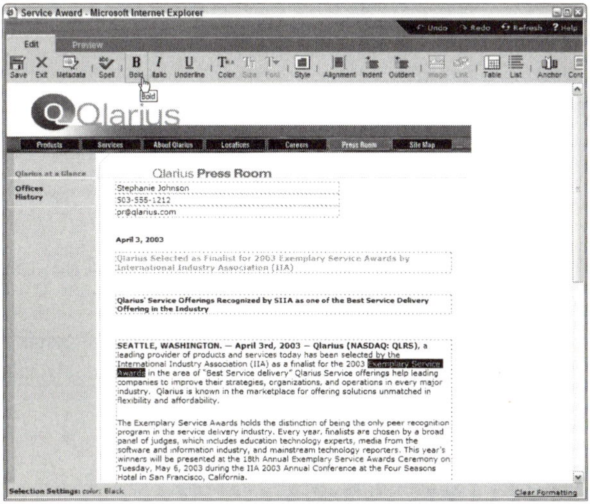

Figure 4-2: With in-context contribution, you can create and edit content in the same format as it will appear on the Web site.

The upside of this is that it's a lot more intuitive for users to contribute content — they know where the content will go and how it will look. The downside is that in a world of reusable content, what you see is a bit misleading. The content may not always end up looking the same as in the authoring environment. For most users, the upside far outweighs the downside.

Drag-and-drop

Some of the content on your site may actually be in the form of documents — things like Word documents and Adobe PDFs. Most content management systems include a browser-based interface for uploading documents, but there is an easier way.

Using standard Web protocols, you can make your content management repository look just like a file system, as shown in Figure 4-3. You create your content in your program of choice (such as Microsoft Word, Adobe Photoshop, and so on). Then, to upload the document, you browse this virtual file system just as you would browse your local machine and drag-and-drop the content into the right folder. For managing documents, it doesn't get much easier than that.

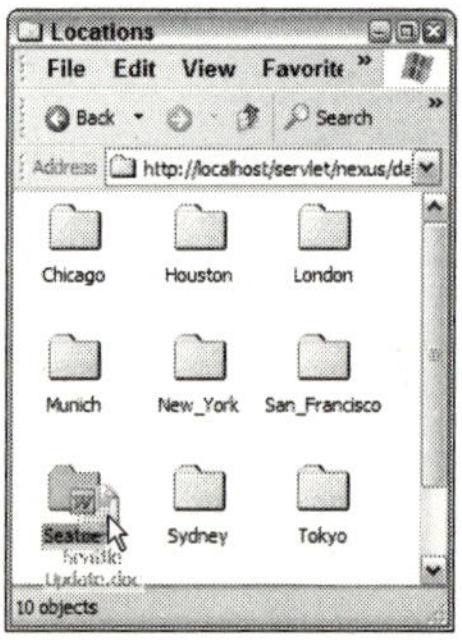

Figure 4-3: Adding content to a content management system can be as easy as dropping content on a "virtual folder."

Converting Documents

What do you do if you have a bunch of content in documents (like Word docs or Excel spreadsheets) that you want to post on your site, but you want them to be presented as HTML and contained within your standard navigation and site look and feel?

This is where document conversion comes into play. Some content management systems can actually convert one document format into another. That Excel spreadsheet you just uploaded could be automatically transformed into HTML so that it blends right in with the rest of the content on your site.

Another common need is to transform common document types into PDFs. Perhaps you want to make it easy for anyone to view the documents (PDF is pretty much universal these days) or maybe you want to let people view the content but not make changes to it (as you could if you got a source Word document).

Some content management systems can actually transform common document types automatically into PDF format. Just think what a timesaver this could be — instead of spending valuable time saving your latest meeting minutes as a PDF, you could just quickly save the source Word document and let the system do the rest. Pretty handy.

Chapter 5

Managing Content

In This Chapter

- Versioning content
- Checking content in and out
- Moving content through a process
- Managing links and images
- Searching, staging, and aging content

Much of what you use a content management system for falls under the category of "managing" content.

Think of your content management system as a library. You have a process for procuring new books and a process for managing the books. I've already talked about how a content management system procures new content (refer to Chapter 4). In this chapter, I talk a bit about how content is actually managed.

The Content Repository

When content is added to a CMS, it is stored in a *repository*. Typically the repository is either a database, a file system (like the folders on your personal computer), or some combination of both. The important thing to know about a repository is that it's the central storage point for your content. Once you get content into the repository, either by importing existing content or authoring new content, you have a lot more control over what you can do with it.

Library services

One of the main benefits of storing content in a repository is that the content can be shared among a bunch of people. This feature makes it a lot more efficient for teams to collaborate on the Web site. But the feature also introduces a problem — how do you make sure that different members of the team don't accidentally overwrite changes others have made by working on the same page at the same time?

This is where *library services* come into play. Just as only one person can check out a book at the same time at your local library, library services within a content management system ensure that only one person can work on a piece of content at any given time. Content authors check out content to make changes to it; when they're done, they check the content back in, thereby making it available to other content authors.

Versioning

Another benefit of using a repository that's managed with library services is that content can be *versioned,* as shown in Figure 5-1. Versioning is fairly straightforward — every time a content author checks a piece of content back into the repository, the system can create a new version of that content. In other words, instead of overwriting the previous version of the content, the system actually stores another copy of the content with the updates and tracks which version was created when and by whom. This feature makes it possible to go back to a previous version in the case of a mistake, or if you need to find out what content was on your site at a given time in the past.

Roll-back

Roll-back is the "undo" command of a content management system. Let's say you just made a change to a press release that's about to be published. As you review your changes, you notice that you messed up and that the previous version is actually the right way to go. Instead of making the changes to the content again, roll-back makes it possible to "undo" your changes and go back to a previous version.

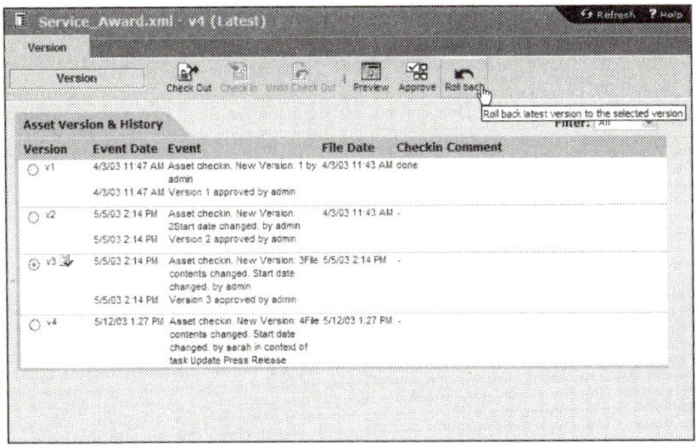

Figure 5-1: Versioning makes it possible to track changes to content over time and to roll back to previous versions.

Workflow

A *workflow* system can help you efficiently move content through the creation and editing process, as shown in Figure 5-2. A workflow system enables Web teams to manage all of the development, writing, editing, and approval steps for Web site assets.

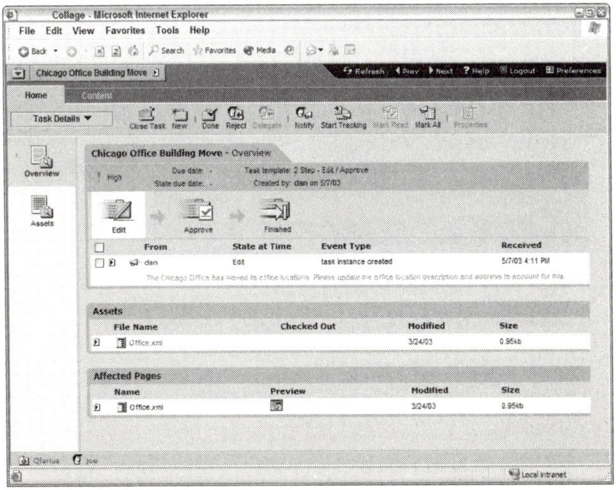

Figure 5-2: Workflow can help streamline the content management process.

Typically, project managers can define as many different types of tasks as necessary, and as many different *workflow states* (or stages of the process) as necessary to support the workflow process.

For example, robust workflow systems offer much more than basic routing of content, such as:

- Tailored workflow processes for different types of content and different user types
- Automatic notification of workflow assignments
- Tracking and notification of task due dates
- Task delegation (in case someone gets sick, fired, thrown in jail, and so on)

TIP

Many workflow systems offer much more functionality than I describe in the preceding bulleted list. Think carefully about what your organization needs and, perhaps more importantly, will actually use, and then look for a system that matches your needs.

WARNING!

A quick note about workflow: Often, organizations seemingly hope that implementing a workflow system will magically turn dysfunctional processes into functional ones. Painful experience has shown that workflow systems only make your organizational processes more efficient — not better. If your processes are dysfunctional *before* a workflow system, chances are a workflow system will simply help you be more swiftly dysfunctional.

Keys to success

The following tips may help you put in place workflow processes that make sense and actually help:

- **Don't use workflow for workflow's sake.** People tend not to like the restrictions of process. So, if you don't have a good reason for a structured process, don't use one. Later in this chapter, I introduce a "pragmatic approach" for getting a lot of the benefits of workflow when structure isn't really needed.
- **If you can't outline your process on paper, you won't be able to do it in a workflow tool.** Start by diagramming

your processes on paper or on a white board. After you've done that, then you can transpose the processes to your workflow engine.

- **Balance, balance, balance.** Keep the goals of the workflow in mind — are you implementing workflow to enforce a process for compliance reasons? Or are you doing it to make things work more smoothly? Do you want to rigidly track due dates? By keeping these goals in mind, you'll be better prepared to design a workflow system that actually works for your organizations.

If you follow these tips, you'll ensure greater benefits from a workflow system.

Taking a pragmatic approach to workflow

Different types of content may require different processes. In fact, some types of content may not require structured workflow at all. Instead, they may be well suited to a simple approval process. A good content management system will provide you with tools for both sophisticated workflow and ad-hoc approval, as shown in Figure 5-3.

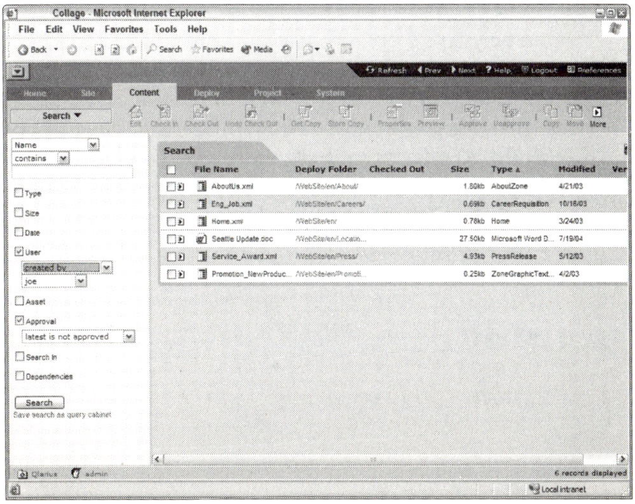

Figure 5-3: If you need only a basic approval workflow, perhaps an ad-hoc approach will best suit your needs.

Ad-hoc approval provides you with a means for rapidly approving content for publishing outside of a structured process. Ad-hoc approval should make it easy to rapidly find all the content in the system that requires approval and can make it simple to quickly mark the appropriate content to be approved.

So, how do you determine which approach is best for a given piece of content? This simple guide will help:

- **Structured workflow:** Structured workflow is best used when you want to enforce a step-by-step process for the content lifecycle, especially if you have to comply with strict regulatory guidelines.
- **Ad-hoc approval:** When you aren't so concerned about enforcing a process but want to automate the approval process, an ad-hoc approval process is likely your best bet.

Automation

Face it, workflow is boring. Who wakes up in the morning, looks in the mirror, and proclaims, "Woo hoo, I get to go edit and approve some content today. Sure am glad I'm part of a workflow"? People tend to resist process. So, whenever possible, make the process a transparent part of performing common tasks.

One way to do so is to use automatic workflow generation. This approach transfers the burden of starting a workflow process from the user to an administrator. Instead of a user determining which workflow process a piece of content should go into, who it should be assigned to, and so on, the administrator sets up some business rules that are used to automatically initiate a workflow process and assign the appropriate users to the task.

The irony of all this is that by *hiding* the details of the process, your users are more likely to *follow* the process.

Link Management

Hyperlinks (or simply *links*) tie the different pages of your site together. A single page may have dozens of links to other pages on your site and even pages on other sites somewhere else on the Web.

Few things are as annoying as clicking on a link only to find out that the link is "broken" — that the page it refers to no longer exists, or has moved. If you want to lose the attention of your site visitors fast, make sure to have broken links on your site.

Despite the obvious need to avoid broken links, recent studies have shown that most sites still contain many broken links — often they're found directly on the main page of the site. How do you avoid this?

The good news is that a good content management system makes it very easy to stay on top of the links on your site. Specifically, a good CMS should

- **Track any *internal links* (links that point from one page on your site to another).** Any time something is done that would break a link (content is deleted, moved, and so on), the system either rectifies the problem or notifies a user that there may be a problem.
- **Report on the status of *external links* (links that point to a page outside of your own site).** You should be able to tell your content management system to check periodically on the health of external links and report any issues.

Figure 5-4 shows an example of link validation.

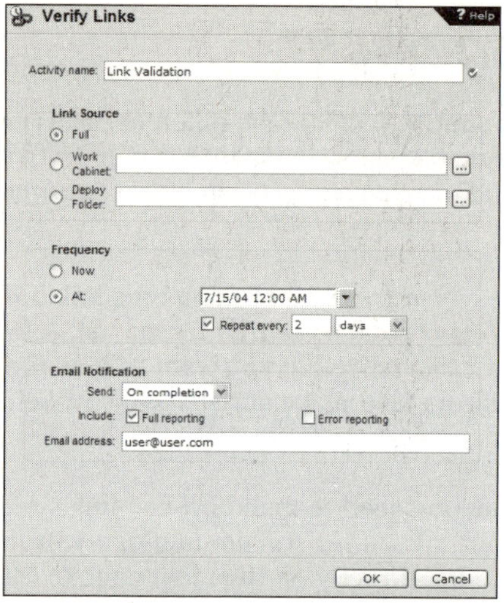

Figure 5-4: A CMS should make regularly validating internal and external links easy to do.

Image Management

In many ways, images should be managed like any other piece of content (see Figure 5-5). Images need to be versioned, approved, published, and so on. In other ways, images are unique. For one, images are often shared among different pages on a site. As such, they need to be easily found so that users can easily include them in content they are authoring.

To easily find images, you need to be able to associate *metadata* (such as keywords, description, and so on) with an image so that a simple search will find the right images. Additionally, your content management system should have the capability of showing you image *thumbnails* (scaled-down versions of an image) so that you can quickly browse through lots of images and find the right one.

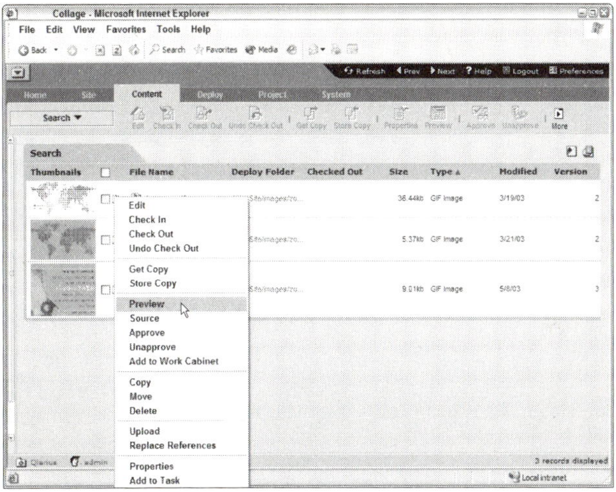

Figure 5-5: Images are an important type of Web site content.

Searching

The content management process can be a real pain if you don't have a good way of finding content in the repository. Good search capabilities are critical, especially as the amount of content on your site increases.

When evaluating a content management system, take some time to understand how a user will go about finding content within the repository. A good content management system makes it simple for a user to perform common searches, and ideally makes it easy to save common searches (such as "show me all the unapproved content on the site") in order to save time on repetitive tasks (see Figure 5-6).

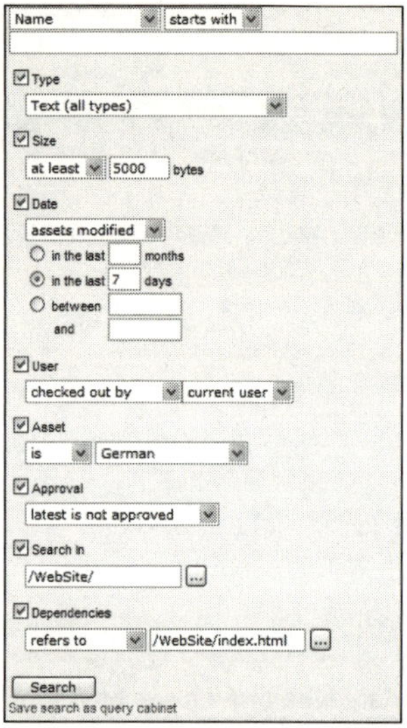

Figure 5-6: Your content management system makes finding that needle in a haystack a breeze.

Staging and Aging

Some types of content have a lifespan. For example, an employee benefit document is pertinent and valid for about a year. Your content management system can make it easy to specify when a piece of content should go live and when it needs to be taken off a site. That way, your HR manager can update the yearly benefits document in September, mark it to go live on January 1, and specify that it needs to be automatically removed from the site at the end of the year. Not only does this save a lot of time, but it also helps to ensure that only fresh, relevant content is available on your site. Figure 5-7 shows an example.

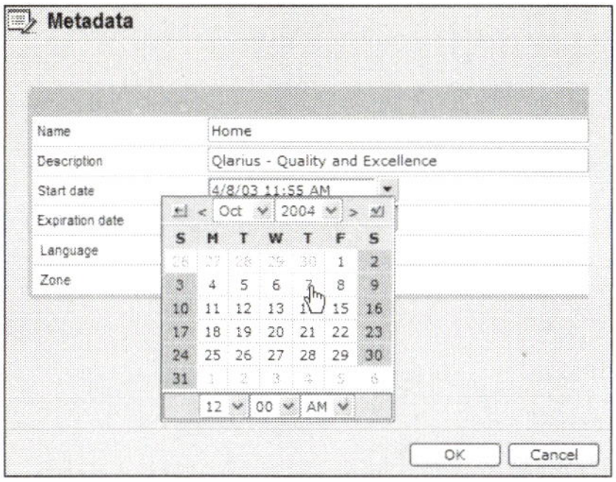

Figure 5-7: Content, like cheese, needs to be staged and aged for best results.

Dependency Management

Tracking dependencies is like figuring out the complex rules teenagers use to determine who can go out with whom. Unless you have a teenager around to keep tabs on these things, you're smart to turn the job over to a computer.

Your Web site is made up of a bunch of pieces of content that are loosely connected together. Tracking the dependencies of one piece of content on another can be very complicated — especially when you repurpose content across many different pages on your site. When you go to delete an image, how are you to know that deleting that image is going to impact five other pages on your site? Dependency management is critical at this point.

A content management system ought to keep track of all the dependencies between different pieces of content. The system should also make it easy to see a list of all the dependencies so that you can assess the impact of making a change on all the different sections of your site. Figure 5-8 shows a dependency management tool in action.

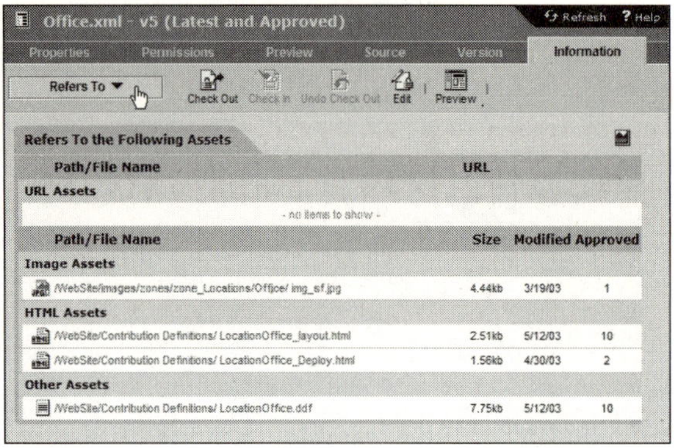

Figure 5-8: Let your CMS keep track of your content co-mingling.

Chapter 6

Publishing Content

In This Chapter

- Understanding content delivery
- Assembling content
- Templating
- Generating pages and sites
- Putting your content out there

Alas, every author dreams of being published. With a good content management system in place, publishing your Web content should be a relatively painless, effortless task.

Content Delivery Basics

Before I can talk much about how content is published, I should step back a bit and take a look at how content is delivered to site visitors. The way the content is delivered will have some impact on *how* the content is published.

In general, you find three different types of approaches to content delivery:

- Static
- Dynamic
- Semi-dynamic

The following sections explain these types of approaches in some detail.

Static content

Using an example rooted in the physical world to explain the different types of content delivery approaches may be helpful here.

Imagine for a moment that you're a travel agent. As a service to your customers, you publish an extremely well-written, informative travel newsletter. The purpose of the newsletter is to inform customers about general travel tips and to introduce them to different regions of the world. You publish the newsletter every two weeks and make it available for anyone who comes to your office. Every person gets exactly the same newsletter, and the newsletters are printed in advance. Getting a newsletter is simple. A customer says: "Hey, I'd like a newsletter," and you pick it up and hand it to them.

Much of the content on the Web is similar to this newsletter. This type of content is called *static content*. Static content shares several characteristics with the newsletter:

- **Already created.** The content is generated in advance of the moment someone accesses it.
- **One size fits all.** Everyone who requests the content gets the same version.
- **Controlled by the publisher.** The content doesn't change until the publisher changes it.

The main benefit of serving static content is that doing so is very fast. It doesn't take much time or many system resources to fetch a page and send it to the site visitor.

The downside of static content is that it isn't well suited for content that changes very frequently or content that is *personalized* (tailored to a particular user's interests or needs). That's where dynamic content comes in.

Dynamic content

Back to the example of the travel agent newsletter. . . . Imagine that someone walks into your travel agency and asks you to print up a list of all the fares from Tulsa to Tuscany. Printing up fare charts for all possible route combinations in advance would be terribly inefficient. Instead, when someone asks you to print a list, you get the latest fares for their specific route and then print a list specifically for the customer.

Well, dynamic content is similar. Fully dynamic pages on the Web don't really exist until they are requested. When information is requested, a script on the server goes into action and gathers the requested information, assembles it into a page, and sends it to the site visitor.

TIP

The benefits of this approach are pretty clear — *dynamic content* makes it possible to present a highly tailored experience to site visitors, complete with the latest information.

The downside is that dynamic pages take many more system resources to generate and are typically more complex to manage. In order to have dynamic pages that respond quickly, you have to have robust hardware and typically a more complex site design in order to decrease the difficulty of presenting a dynamic page.

REMEMBER

Because dynamic content requires more resources and can be a bit slow, few pages on the Web are *truly* dynamic. Most pages that appear to be dynamic are actually semi-dynamic.

Semi-dynamic content

So, back to the travel agent newsletter example. Because you are such a great travel agent, you provide your customers with *travel packs* — a collection of information with travel advice, maps, brochures, and so on. To be efficient, you prepare most of the pack (advice, maps, and brochures) in advance. When a customer requests a pack, you quickly print out their custom itinerary based on their desired travel, add it to the pack, and they're good to go.

Semi-dynamic pages are similar to the travel pack. Most of the page is assembled and ready to go before anyone comes along and requests it. Only the sections of the page that need to be customized (like a stock quote, customized greeting, and so on) are dynamically generated. The pre-assembled portion of the page is merged with the dynamic portion, and the page is delivered to a site visitor.

Semi-dynamic pages provide the benefits of tailored dynamic content without as high an impact on system resources and with less design difficulty.

Mix and match

So, which type of content is best for your Web site? You don't actually have to choose a single type of content for your entire site. Various types of content call for different approaches — a press release will likely be static, whereas a search results page has to include dynamic content. You will most likely want to maximize your site's speed — and minimize your site's need for system resources — by using dynamic and semi-dynamic content only where necessary, and static content everywhere else.

TIP: If you're evaluating content management systems, look for one that allows you the flexibility to mix and match static and dynamic content.

Assembling Your Content

One of the most important phases of a publishing process is *content assembly*. This phase is when all sorts of magic starts happening:

- **Structured content is assembled.** If you are using structured content, the different parts of content (for example, headline, body, and so on) are brought together to produce the final output. At the same time, the content can be merged with formatting elements (such as font, size, color, and so on) (refer to Chapter 2).
- **Documents are converted.** Documents may be transformed from one format (for example, Word docs) to another (for example, HTML or PDF) (refer to Chapter 4).
- **Links are created.** Content relationships previously stored as database references are turned into HTML links (refer to Chapter 5).
- **Site structure may be created.** The folder structure used to manage the content may be rearranged to a structure better suited for a live Web site (refer to Chapter 5).

- **Graphics are applied.** Navigation, branding, and other graphical elements are applied to content.

Once assembled, the content can be published to its ultimate destination.

In a run-time content management system, the content assembly happens when the content is requested by a site visitor, whereas in a design-deploy system, the content is assembled at the time of publishing (refer to Chapter 3). In either case, the process is very similar.

Templating

Templates are often used to merge form and content. Content management *templating* is basically a glorified mail merge. (A *mail merge* is a tool that allows you to write a form letter and then automatically generate multiple copies of the letter, each with a different recipient pulled from an address list.) A template for a mail merge might look like this:

```
"Company Name"<Line Break>
Attention: "First Name" "Last Name"<Line Break>
"Street Address"<Line Break>
"City", "State" "Zip Code"
```

The various placeholders in the template designate where different elements of the address should be placed. Pretty straightforward, no?

Conceptually, content management templates are very similar. A simple content management template may look something like this:

```
<$.insert="navigation-bar"><br>
Welcome to my site!<p>
<b><$.insert="news-headline"></b><br>
<font color="red"><$.insert="news-
summary"></font>
```

If this all looks like gibberish, don't worry, it is. Understanding the basic concept is much more important than the specifics here — especially given the fact that the templating language I just used probably doesn't exist.

While templating languages differ significantly, they all hold a few things in common. Every templating language can be used to:

- Merge content with form
- Assemble different pieces of content together
- Assemble pages or parts of pages

Although all templating languages do the same basic things, they differ dramatically in their sophistication and complexity. Before purchasing a content management system, take a quick look to see what functionality is offered in the templating language and how complex it will be to learn to write templates in the language.

Generating Your Pages and Site

Although I briefly touched on page generation in the preceding section on templates, the topic is important enough to go into it in some more detail.

In order to assemble your content into something meaningful, the content management system needs to generate pages, site sections, and ultimately your entire site. This process includes a lot of separate specific events. In the following sections, I focus on the key points.

Page generation

At its simplest, page generation is simply a matter of taking an existing HTML page (created in Dreamweaver, FrontPage, or some other HTML editor) and publishing it with the appropriate links to other pages on the site.

But page generation can do a lot more than that. To illustrate this, take a look at a sample page from a fictitious company, Qlarius (Figure 6-1).

Look at the Qlarius page-component parts. (This is a lot like high school biology, except that you aren't dissecting some creature soaked in formaldehyde.)

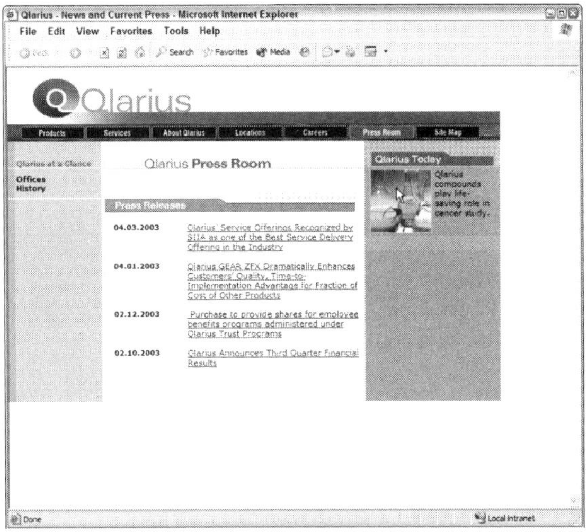

Figure 6-1: A sample page from Qlarius, some company I just made up.

At the top of the page is a branding bar. This section of the page is managed as a *discrete element* (a separate chunk) so that you can change it in one place and your change will be reflected across all pages that use it.

Down the left side of the page is a navigation bar. This section of the page is also managed as a discrete element (notice a trend here) for the same reasons stated before. The difference here is that the navigation bar changes based on the section of the site the visitor is in. To make this happen, the page generation system has to be intelligent enough to figure out what the appropriate navigation is for the page.

The main section of the page is a list of recent press releases. This is the result of a query — basically a bit of programming code that asks the system to give it a list of the most recent press releases. Queries can be really easy to build, or really complex — in part based on what you're trying to do, but also dependent on how much your content management system is able to help you. So how does that work? See the next section.

Queries

Very few people think it's fun to build queries. Most queries are built using a language called SQL, sometimes pronounced "sequel."

SQL makes creating queries fairly easy, but they still aren't the most fun thing you can do with your time. For starters, in order to write a SQL query, you have to understand the structure of the data you are querying. So, a good content management system will make it possible to query your content without understanding SQL or the structure of your data.

Content management systems have to make some tradeoffs. On the one hand, they can make queries extremely easy to create, but that usually comes at the expense of flexibility. Or they can make it really flexible and customizable at the expense of ease of use.

The best systems take a middle-of-the-road approach and make creating queries pretty simple, but still give you the flexibility to do nearly everything you would ever want to do. You may notice that I say "nearly everything." So, what about those things you may want to do that aren't covered by the CMS functionality? That's where SQL comes back into the picture. If you want to do something fancy that the system doesn't support natively, the system should allow you to use raw SQL to get the job done.

Pagelets

In this chapter, I talk about how pages can be assembled. But what if you don't want to publish complete pages all the time — say, if you're going to assemble pages using a different system (like a portal server) or scripting language (like ASP, JSP, or PHP). Well, the same principles that apply to pages also apply to *sections* of pages.

Sometimes these sections of pages are called "pagelets." (The name pagelet doesn't make a lot of sense. If a pagelet is just a portion of a page, then shouldn't a piglet be just a portion of a pig?) In any case, a *pagelet* is a self-contained bit of content that will be used to create a page at some point in time.

Publishing destinations

One of the great things about getting control of your content is that it makes publishing your content to any number of different places much easier. Perhaps you post a press release to your public Web site, your intranet, a partner's site, a company extranet, maybe even your personal Web site if you're one of those types who doesn't seem to be able to leave work behind.

The challenge of publishing content to lots of different places is that each destination may require different formatting (that is, the way it looks) or may require the content to be in a unique format (that is, how it is structured). Your content management system needs to be adept at publishing content to a variety of destinations, in a variety of formats.

Here are just a few examples of the different destinations you may want to publish your content:

- **Web server:** Typically, you publish content to a Web server as HTML in the form of pages or parts of pages, sometimes called pagelets (see the "Pagelets" sidebar in this chapter for more info).
- **Databases:** Sometimes you may want to publish your content to another database, for example, if you've written a custom Web application or have some other system that uses a database to access Web content.
- **Portal server:** Portal servers can use content in a variety of formats. Depending on the server and your needs, you may publish the content as XML, HTML, or directly to a database where the portal server will access it for delivery.
- **Raw XML:** I can think of several reasons you may want to publish content in raw XML, and I'm not going to talk about them here, other than to mention that the reasons exist. If you're concerned about XML (and you know who you are), make sure that you select a CMS that makes it easy to publish content in an XML format.
- **WAP servers:** Don't get WAP confused with WHAM. You may hear either one when you swat a fly with a book, but it really depends on the size of the book. Okay, here's the

real difference: One sang songs about wake-up calls, and the other stands for Wireless Access Protocol. If you guessed that WAP is the one that stands for Wireless Access Protocol, you are indeed correct. If you guessed WHAM, it's time to break out of the '80s.

WAP (Wireless Access Protocol)

Now that we have the bullet list in the previous section out of the way, I can talk seriously about WAP. WAP is simply the protocol that is used to send content to wireless devices, like cellphones. WAP sends content to wireless devices using WML, a specialized version of HTML designed specifically for wireless devices. As you may figure, content sent to wireless devices tends to have less fancy formatting and is usually broken down into chunks that are more easily read on those luxuriously large cellphone screens. In any case, if you want to publish your content for viewing on the small screen, you need a system that will help you get it in the right format.

Here's where this gets fun. Depending on your needs, a single site may comprise more than one of these destinations. Your CMS needs to do a good job of supporting different delivery methods, or you could have a real headache on your hands.

The Publishing Process

Whew, I've used a lot of paper and print discussing all the things that go into publishing content, but I haven't actually talked about the *process* of publishing the content. Imagine that. Well, here we are.

Setup

Before you can actually publish the content, there's a little setup that has to happen in any system, as shown in Figure 6-2. You have to tell the system where you want to publish the content, which protocol (that is, geeky Web transport system) you want to use, give it passwords, and so on. That's at its simplest, and if your requirements are simple, that may be *all* you need to do. More complex publishing operations may require a bit more setup. Of course, a content management system with more complex options is always a good idea, especially if the system makes them fairly simple.

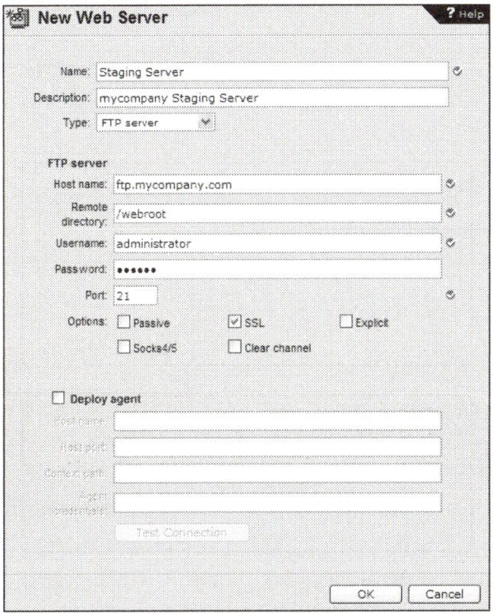

Figure 6-2: A publishing setup.

Mapping

You may want to map content from one structure in your content management system to a different structure on, for example, a Web server (see Figure 6-3). Perhaps you have the content organized in a way that makes sense to internal CMS users, but want to organize the content in a way that makes sense to your customers on your live site. Some content management systems can actually map one structure to another, giving you the best of both worlds.

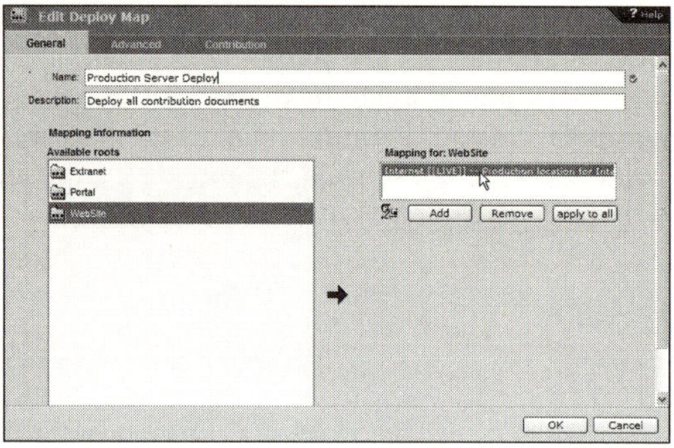

Figure 6-3: Mapping content structures.

Database publishing

I've already gone over some of the reasons why you may want to publish content to a database. The actual process of publishing content from one database to another can be a real drag. Some content management systems provide utilities that make the publishing process much easier, as shown in Figure 6-4. If you think you may want to publish to a database, save yourself the headache and make sure to keep this in mind up front when considering a CMS.

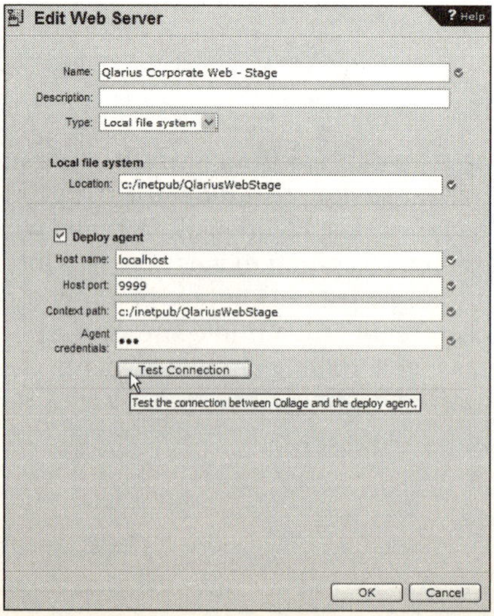

Figure 6-4: Setting up to publish to another database.

Multi-destination publishing

TIP

If you're going to publish content to multiple destinations, or you're going to publish different sections of your site using different publishing rules, it's always nice if your content management system helps you do this in a straightforward way.

Actually Publishing

Okay! I've dragged you through all the nuts and bolts and now it's time to actually hit the publish button. This may be the easiest part of managing your content. That is, if everything goes smoothly. If everything goes smoothly, you can sit back and nibble on some bonbons as you watch your content silently stream to the wonderful Web world. (Almost poetic, isn't it?)

I hate to break into your blissful dream, but what happens if things don't go right? Even in the best systems with the best setup, problems arise. That's why it's vital, critical, essential, key, and yes even crucial that your content management gives you some feedback during the publishing process (Figure 6-5). That way, as you're eating your bonbons, you can keep tabs on the publishing progress.

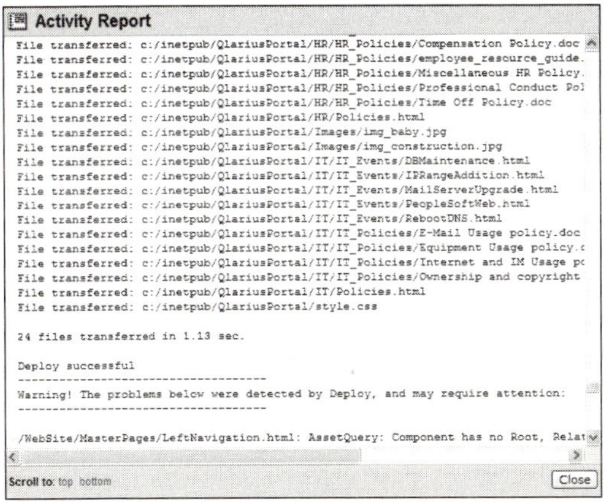

Figure 6-5: Your publishing system should tell you what goes right and what goes wrong.

Of course, it's always swell if the system tells you something more than "publish failed." Ideally, the system should tell you what it was able to do before it failed, when it failed, and why it failed.

Further, recognizing that all failures aren't of the same magnitude, there are fatal failures, colossal failures, giant failures, major failures, failures, small failures, and seemingly insignificant failures. Based on the magnitude of the failure, you may want the publishing process to continue with its work and then go back later to fix the minor failures.

The bottom line is, the more insight and control you have when it comes to publishing failures, the lower your stress level will be. I make no guarantees that your stress level will be lower with a content management system. I am quite certain, though, that content management systems have little to do with male pattern baldness.

Scheduled publishing

Remember when I talked about eating bonbons while waiting for a publishing process to complete? Well, wouldn't it be even better if you could be at home, nestled in your cozy bed instead? That's where *scheduled publishing* comes in (Figure 6-6).

Once you know that a publishing process is working, why not just tell the system when you want it to happen and let the system deal with it. When you wake up in the morning, you can grab your pint of Ben and Jerry's (hey, this isn't a diet book after all), check your e-mail, and see how things went while you were sleeping.

Scheduled deploys (as scheduled publishing events are called) are also handy when you want to publish your site frequently, say every 15 minutes or so.

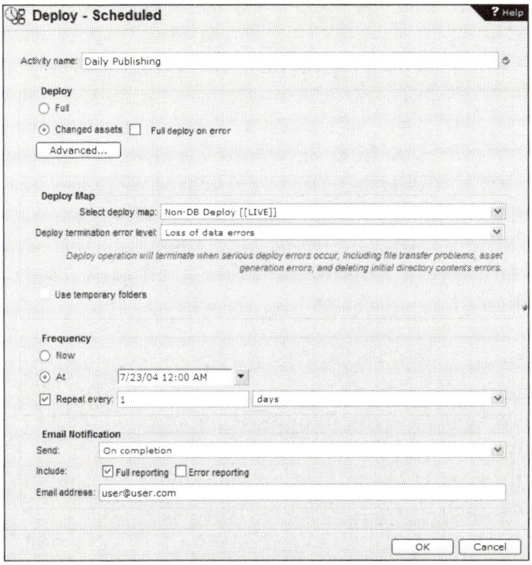

Figure 6-6: Save yourself some hassle and schedule your site publishing.

Incremental publishing

What do you do if it takes an hour to publish your entire site, but you want to publish your site every 15 minutes? No, this isn't a Mensa quiz, so don't spend too much time trying to figure out the math on that one.

There's really only one way around the problem: You have to speed up the publishing process. You could throw some more hardware at the problem (figuratively speaking, of course), but that's expensive and likely won't solve the problem. Besides, there's a much easier way.

What if instead of publishing your *entire* site every time you publish the site, you actually just publish the things that have changed since the last time you published the site? Now say *that* really fast! Such a publishing phenomenon is called an *incremental publishing event.* This handy way of publishing things is actually rather complex.

Here's a quick example of where the complexity comes in: Say that you've added a fresh news article to your site. It's easy enough for the system to figure out that you just added something new and that it should be published. But, say that you also have a page on your site that includes a query that lists the titles of the latest five news articles. Technically, the page displaying the last five news articles doesn't change when you add the new article. The list of the query results changes, but the static portions of the page really don't, so why bother publishing all the unchanged elements again?

That's where your content management system needs to be really smart. The CMS needs to anticipate that the results of the query will have changed based on the content that was just added. The process is sort of like telepathy, but not as creepy. If you think you'll need to update your site incrementally, make sure that the system you're going to use is smart enough to figure out everything that needs to be changed.

Chapter 7

Reporting and Auditing

In This Chapter

- Reporting on content changes
- Keeping track of content changes
- Auditing content management activity

With all the changes and activity going on in your content management system, seeing who changed what and when is extremely important. This is especially true if you work for an organization that is highly regulated, such as a financial services firm. Many organizations are required to show exactly when certain changes were made to a Web site. For example, a financial services organization may be required to show that a rate change was posted on the site at any given time.

Whether or not you work in a regulated industry, it's pretty handy to be able to see what happened on your site at a specific time. In this chapter, I give you some examples of the types of things you'll be able to see in your CMS.

Content History

Content history is just what it sounds like — the history of the content. (Yes, you're absolutely right; I'm never going to get a job writing definitions for a dictionary.) For any asset, you should be able to see each of the asset revisions, who made changes to the asset, to whom the asset was assigned, when it was published, and so on. The content management system should make it easy to get at all the data surrounding the asset so that if you need to check into an asset's shady past, you don't have to look far (see Figure 7-1).

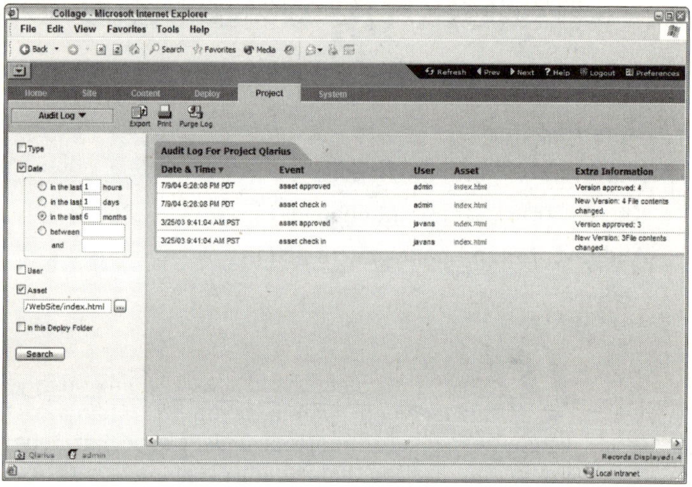

Figure 7-1: Keep tabs on your content.

Publishing History

If you want to find out what was published when, but you don't know exactly which assets to look for, publishing history is a handy thing. Publishing history should tell you exactly what was published during any publishing event. It should keep a record of what failed, what succeeded, and when various pieces of content were published (see Figure 7-2).

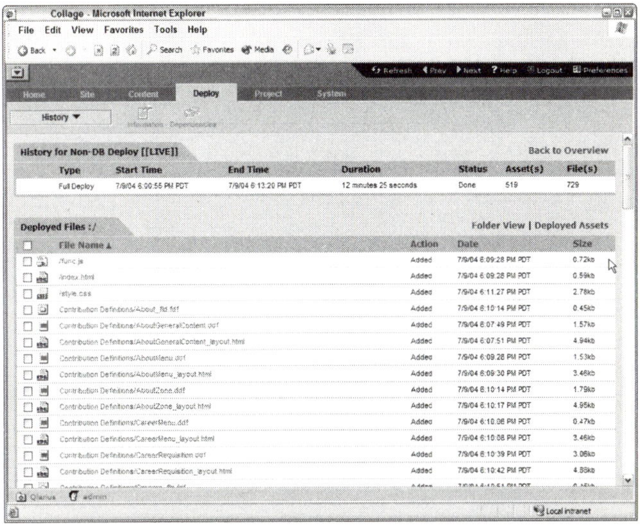

Figure 7-2: You should be able to quickly see exactly what was published to your site.

Miscellaneous History

You may want to keep track of several other things that don't fall neatly under either the asset or publishing history categories (see Figure 7-3). Here are just a few:

- Who logged in and when
- Failed logins
- System uptime
- When a workflow task was completed
- Anything that happened on a particular date

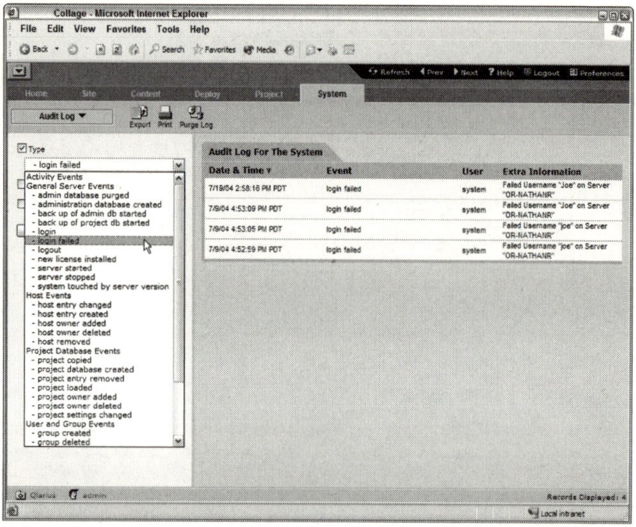

Figure 7-3: Some content management systems make it easy to keep tabs of just about anything that happens in the system.

Export History

A good content management system should enable you to get access to history information rapidly — preferably through the same interface you use to manage the content. But, there are times when exporting the historical information out of the content management system makes sense. For example:

- **Evaluation using another application.** Perhaps you want to analyze the historical data using Microsoft Excel, a database, or a graphical reporting tool.
- **Backup to another system.** Historical information can be invaluable in the case of an audit, lawsuit, or some other such delightful event. Make sure the CMS you choose provides an export feature so that you can back up or analyze content history in detail.

Chapter 8

System and User Management

In This Chapter

- Securing your content
- Keeping important assets backed up
- Managing users

This chapter focuses on things that appeal mostly to system administrators. These things are generally mundane features that most people don't like to think about a whole lot. It just so happens, though, that these mundane things can make or break your content management implementation, so you had better pay attention.

Keeping Things Secure

Security means different things to different people depending on their title and area of focus. In every case, however, security is the focus of ensuring that the right people have access to the right content and functionality at the right time. The fundamental principle of security is user management.

User management

In order to manage who can see and do what, you need to be able to keep track of who has access to the system. This is what *user management* does.

User management isn't exactly the most exciting thing on earth, so it's important that your content management system makes it as easy as possible to manage users efficiently (leaving you to more important things). Most systems will break user management into a few pieces, as I discuss in the following sections.

User profiles

User profiles define the actual users of the system. An administrator usually assigns each user a user name, password, e-mail address — you know, the basic properties that you expect a user to have (see Figure 8-1).

Many applications (e-mail servers, HR applications, and so on) require the same sort of user profiles as a content management system. Perhaps your organization already has a user management system in place (sometimes called an LDAP, or "el-dap" system). If so, look for a content management system that's able to use the user profiles already stored in the LDAP system so that you don't have to manually key them all in.

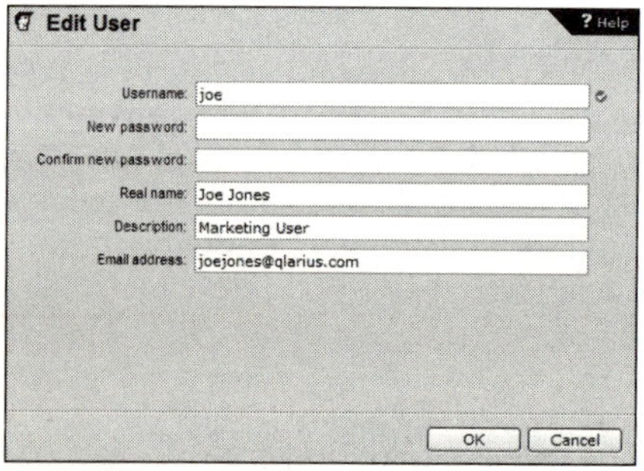

Figure 8-1: A simple user profile.

User groups and/or roles

Managing users one-by-one can be terribly tedious and inefficient. That's where user groups or roles come in. When managing a group of users, a system administrator can assign properties to a group. From there, all members of that group inherit those rights unless they're explicitly overridden for an individual user. This makes managing large numbers of users a lot easier (see Figure 8-2).

Rights and privileges

Many systems define certain categories of things that a user may want to do or see. A user (or group) can then be given rights (sometimes called *privileges*) to see or do those things (Figure 8-3). Here are a few examples:

- Infrequent users of the system may be given rights to create new content, but not to delete it.
- Frequent users may be given rights to create, edit, modify, and approve content, but may not get the rights to publish content.
- Power users, such as your bad self, may be given rights to do absolutely anything in the system.

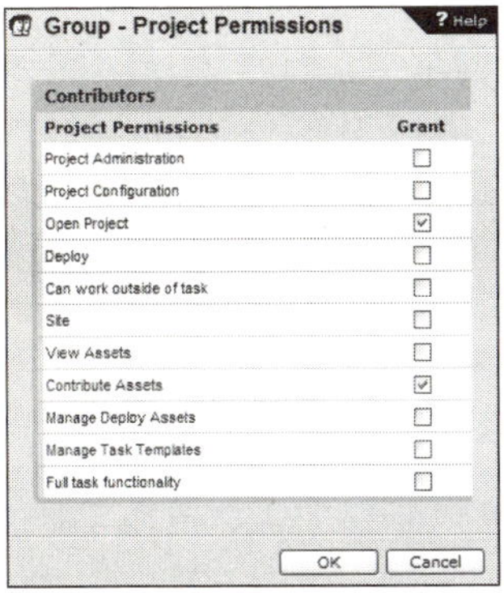

Figure 8-2: A group of contributors are granted certain rights to the system.

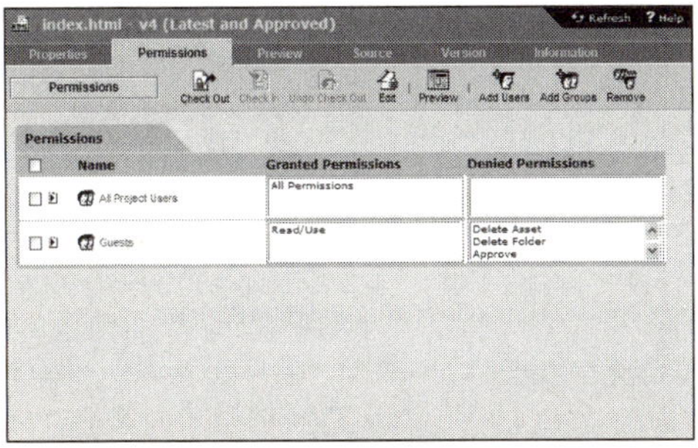

Figure 8-3: Look for a CMS that's able to restrict what users can see and do in the system.

A user's rights ought to impact both what they can *do* and what they can *see*. The latter is especially important, as it helps make the system easier to use.

Backing Up Important Assets

A few thousand words ago, I said that your Web sites are mission critical. Since your sites are mission critical, you need to make sure that you have regular backups of your system (see Figure 8-4).

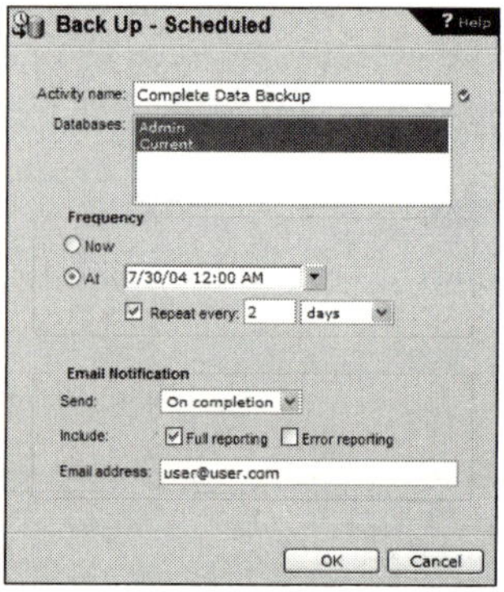

Figure 8-4: Back up your data regularly to avoid catastrophe.

I'm not talking about the ability to roll back a piece of content — that's an entirely different issue. What I am talking about is the kind of backup you need if something goes terribly, terribly wrong. Like if a family of gerbils decided to make your server their home and used the CPU fan as their fun little exercise wheel.

With a content management system, you should be able to frequently back up your entire content management implementation, including:

- All the content, including all versions
- All the metadata
- Workflow definitions
- History and audit information
- User accounts and permissions

With sufficient backup features, you can get a crashed Web site up and running again without a major freakout. Minor freakouts are perfectly acceptable.

Part III

The Part of Tens

The 5th Wave By Rich Tennant

"FOR US, IT WAS TOTAL INTEGRATION OR NOTHING. FOR INSTANCE- AT THIS TERMINAL ALONE I CAN GET DEPARTMENTAL DATA, PRINTER AND STORAGE RESOURCES, ESPN, HOME SHOPPING NETWORK AND THE MOVIE CHANNEL."

In this part . . .

You discover a few ways to make sure that your content management implementation lives up to its potential.

Chapter 9

Ten Best CMS Practices

In This Chapter

- Achieving content management success
- Keeping things neat, tidy, and sunburn free
- Preventing accidents

In a recent survey of "well-known" sites, Jupiter Media reported that 1 in 7 home pages (that's over 14 percent) failed a basic link-integrity test. And these are "well-known" sites?

Some of us (ahem, most of us) got a tad too excited about all the nifty things the Web can do and ignored the basics. After all, how many sites have you been to that greet you with a nice personalized greeting, yet are so blasted difficult to navigate that you leave the site cursing?

So, I'd like to suggest ten best practices that, if followed, will help you move toward content management nirvana. Please don't thank me now. A simple box of assorted chocolates from La Maison du Chocolat will do just fine.

Stick to the Fundamentals

Fundamentals are boring. Yet fundamentals separate the best sites from the also-rans. Google out-Yahoo'd Yahoo by sticking to the fundamentals. eBay isn't much more than a garage sale — a very well-organized and well-run garage sale, at that.

Before you spend time on fancy personalization, funky three-dimensional navigation, and the like, make sure that your site does what it needs to do. Once you've nailed the fundamentals, you can move on — that is, if sticking to the fundamentals doesn't convince you that your time isn't better spent elsewhere.

Technology Tends to Amplify Organizational Habits

Software doesn't magically change human behavior. Without careful introduction, software usually amplifies human behavior. If an organization is completely dysfunctional, software will sometimes just make it easier to be more efficiently dysfunctional. If you buy software, content management or otherwise, hoping that it will turn your process-loathing colleagues into something other than process-loathing colleagues, there's a good chance you're in for a letdown. You can, however, do a few things to increase your chances of success:

- **Focus on the goal, not the technology.** Users are more likely to adopt new software and processes if they understand the goal and how the software helps them achieve it.
- **Don't force users to do more than they have to.** Automate as much as can be automated. Hide as much as can be hidden. Streamline, streamline, streamline.

An Ounce of Prevention . . .

The Web is replete with examples of organizations that did stupid things that cost them in big ways (usually in the form of money, pain, or embarrassment, or a combination of the three). Some classic examples: hotel rooms in exotic places offered for less than your monthly rent, sophisticated computer equipment being sold for pennies, and classified documents being posted for everyone in the world to see.

Processes need to be in place to lessen the chances that stupid things like these will happen. No matter how good your processes, though, stupid things will happen on occasion. That's why it's good to be prepared for unforeseen stupid things. Prepare a contingency plan to deal with mistakes *before* they happen. You may not anticipate the exact problem, but you can be part way to a solution when the time arises.

Different Users Have Different Needs

Not all users are alike. If you want end-user mutiny on your hands when you introduce a new application, the fastest way to force the mutiny is to treat all users exactly the same.

Before you roll out a new application (and ideally before you even select a new application), take a moment to think about your users. Classify them into groups. Determine their needs, their skills, and their tolerance for new applications. Then make sure to do as much as you can to provide interfaces for each of the different groups that will help them be successful.

Every Project Needs Sponsors

People resist change. We seem to have resistance in our DNA. If you want your content management implementation to be a success, make sure to get the right people on board as soon as possible. Sometimes the right people may seem like the wrong people. Often the people that are most likely to challenge change are exactly the right ones to bring in early in the process. If you can get them to take some ownership in the solution, they'll often turn out to be your best evangelists.

Don't Forget Hygiene

Have you ever had a conversation with someone who was just brilliant, but their breath was so nasty that you could hardly pay attention? The same thing can happen with your Web site. You can have the best content, but if you've forgotten basic hygiene (link checking, content expiration, correct spelling, and so on), you may drive away your customers. Give someone the responsibility to keep track of site hygiene and make sure they have time in the project schedule to get it done.

Design with Usability in Mind

Who cares if you have the coolest content management system in the world if no one can use it? You have to keep usability in mind throughout the entire process. Choosing a usable, intuitive content management system can certainly help, but that is by no means the end of the task. Every design and implementation decision you make can have an impact on how easy it is for users to use the site.

Also, bear in mind that there are two sides to the usability coin. On one side is the issue of learning how to do something; on the other is the ongoing task of doing things once you've learned the system. The simplest user interface isn't necessarily the most usable one for all users.

Share the Wealth

Don't be a content management hog. Sometimes it can be hard to let go of your precious Web site. How can you countenance the thought of giving those Web site newbies, those veritable troglodytes, rights to make changes to your Web site? Just remember, such an attitude will just mean that you have to work longer days and more weekends while the cave dwellers sip mai tais somewhere far away. Take the time to get more people involved. It means less work for you in the long run.

Demonstrate Success Early

As I discuss elsewhere, people tend to resist change. But people also like to share success. So, make sure to demonstrate success early in your content management implementation and then herald it from the mountaintops (or desktop, blacktop, or via your laptop). Spread credit liberally, making sure to give ample credit to everyone who contributed.

Use Sunscreen

With all of this extra time you have on your hands, you should have plenty of time to head down to the beach, or wherever it is you worship the sun, and catch some rays. I highly recommend you use sunscreen.

Chapter 10

Ten Web Basics

While some Web sites can be hugely complex (think Amazon.com), the vast majority of Web sites are actually quite simple — especially when broken down into their component parts. A basic understanding of how Web sites work goes a long way toward understanding how to make the process of managing them a whole lot easier.

Why Is It Called "the Web," Anyway?

Ever wonder how the World Wide Web got its weird name? The Web is made up of millions of computers that are connected using the Internet — basically just a big network. If you were to draw a diagram of these computers, there would be lines crisscrossing the world like a big web. Hence, the World Wide Web.

Why does this matter? Different computers connected to the Internet play different roles in this global network. For the sake of our discussion, we're really only concerned about two of these roles: servers and clients.

- **Servers.** A server contains information that other computers can request. In other words, a server is a computer that has the capability to access and send information to other computers. Simple enough, no?
- **Clients.** Here's a tongue-twister for you: Clients are the consumers of the information that servers serve. Ugh. Let me try again. Client computers request information from server computers.

For example, say that you sit down at your home computer to buy a book, so you type `www.amazon.com` into your Web browser. Your computer (the client) asks another computer (a server computer at `www.amazon.com`) for a Web page.

The Conspicuous Consumer: Web Browsers

Most content on the Web is viewed by using Web browsers like Microsoft Internet Explorer, Netscape Navigator, or Apple Safari. Modern browsers do a lot of things, but at their core, they really do two things: request and display Web content.

When you type `www.amazon.com` into your browser, the Web browser perks up and says "Hey, I need to go get a Web page at `www.amazon.com`." Through a whole lot of really geeky black magic, the Web browser figures out which server (out of the millions on the Web) to ask for the `www.amazon.com` page. Once it finds the right server, the browser requests a copy of the Web page so that it can display the page on the client machine. The server sends the page and any associated content (like the images) to the client computer for viewing.

The server typically sends the client the Web page in HTML (for HyperText Markup Language — I talk some more about HTML in a minute). The browser reads the HTML and formats the page according to the instructions contained within the HTML and its associated files. So, what you see is really your browser's *interpretation* of what the page is supposed to look like. Different browsers interpret HTML differently. As a publisher, you need careful planning to make sure that your Web pages appear as intended in different browsers.

HTML

HyperText Mark-up Language (HTML) is the workhorse of the Web. Most content you view through the Web browser on your computer is formatted using HTML. HTML is a simple language that defines how content should be displayed in a browser. It uses *tags* to specify how various pieces of content should be displayed. For example, let's say that I wanted to make the phrase "this is in italics" show up in italics. In HTML, I would write `<i>this is in italics</i>`. When rendered in the browser, it would look something like this:

> *this is in italics*

HTML includes a slew of pre-defined tags that work just like the `<i>` tag does for italics. The great thing about HTML is that it's fairly easy to understand. The bad thing about HTML is that it can be tedious and cumbersome to implement. Who wants to spend their time putting tags in a document, after all?

Cascading Style Sheets

Cascading Style Sheets (CSS) make HTML a lot more powerful and efficient. Basically, a style sheet gives a page designer more control over how a page looks. Using CSS, designers can specify exactly what font size to use and can even create custom tags that define how content is displayed.

For example, say I'm creating a Web page with a bunch of names that I want to display in blue font. With HTML, I have to tag each name with the font color. But then, what if I want to change the font color? If I use CSS, I can give each name a "class" (basically a custom tag, for example, `<name>`) and then globally specify (or change) the font color for that specific class, saving me work.

Javascript

Many Web pages contain *Javascript* — a lightweight coding language that makes it possible to do all sorts of things like create fancy menus or change the appearance of buttons as you run your mouse over the button. Suffice it to say that Javascript is yet another thing you have to manage as you try to keep your Web site working smoothly.

XML

XML is HTML's smart cousin. Where HTML is all about *show* (how pages are formatted), XML is all about *structure* (what the page, or document, actually contains). Take the following example. Pretend for a minute that you're a machine trained to parse information and you get this bit of HTML:

```
<i>Bill Gates</i>
```

What can you figure out based on the information in the document? Not much. All you know is that the text "Bill Gates" should be formatted in italics. Now, let's say you get this bit of XML passed to you:

```
<person>
<name>Bill Gates</name>
</person>
```

The XML data gives you a lot more information about the structure of the content. From this information, you (remember, you're still a machine) can figure out that you're dealing with a person with the name Bill Gates.

Structured XML makes doing nifty things with the data easier, like transforming it from one structure to another, or exchanging content between systems that may have slightly different ways of dealing with data.

Scripting Languages

Dynamically generated sites usually use some sort of scripting language, such as JSP, ASP, PHP, and so on, to assemble the pages. These languages make it possible to merge both static and dynamic content together in order to present a page to a site visitor. Scripting languages can also be used to perform operations, such as determine what content is best suited for a site visitor based on a set of business rules.

Security

Security is often used to make sure that payment information, such as a credit card number, isn't sent in the Internet equivalent of plain view. But many other types of communications need to be kept secure as well.

Many different methods of Internet security exist. The most widely used is a protocol called SSL, which stands for *Secure Socket Layering* (don't worry, you don't really need to know that). Basically, SSL and other protocols encrypt information as it is sent over the Internet. When information is encrypted, it's jumbled up so that if someone were to intercept the communication, it would look like gibberish. Only a computer with the appropriate electronic "key" can unlock the gibberish to make sense of it.

Flash

Macromedia Flash is a ubiquitous format that is used for creating animations and interactive content for the Web. Flash content is authored using Macromedia Director or other tools and is stored as a binary file, similar to the way a Word document is stored. To view a Flash file, a user needs to have a browser plug-in — basically an extension to the browser — that knows how to read and display the file. The vast majority of computers connected to the Internet are capable of reading Flash files.

Index

• A •

• B •

• C •

• D •

• E •

• F •

• G •

• H •

• I •

Introducing Serena® Collage®

Collage is an award-winning Web content management solution used by organizations throughout the world to manage Web content. Collage presents the following powerful combination of features:

- **Focused on efficiency.** Collage is focused on the challenge of efficiently managing changes to critical Web content.
- **Respects your existing Web sites.** Collage is based on the premise that your organization already has functional, mission-critical Web sites in place. You shouldn't have to re-create those Web sites from scratch to get value from your content management system. Collage rapidly imports existing Web site content and provides scalable control of Web sites within hours of implementation.
- **Respects your existing IT infrastructure.** Collage assumes that you've already invested significant time and money in your IT infrastructure. Collage works with your existing infrastructure and doesn't go about replacing it.
- **Intuitive.** Collage provides intuitive user interfaces that are tailored for different user types, making it easy for you to get your job done quickly.
- **Priced sensibly.** A full Collage implementation is often less than just the yearly maintenance cost for other content management systems.

So, Who Uses Collage?

Collage is used by hundreds of organizations worldwide including educational, government, non-profit, and commercial organizations. To see a partial list of Collage customers, take a look at `http://www.serena.com/collagecustomers`.

Although you'll likely recognize many of the names on this page, you may not know a number of them — Collage isn't so complex that only huge organizations with enormous budgets can use it.

What Benefits Can I Expect?

- **Control.** Collage makes it possible to rapidly gain control of existing Web sites (and any future Web sites you plan on building) through sophisticated, smart site import. Once imported, Collage provides versioning, library services, user rights and security, and workflow capabilities to keep you in control of your content.
- **Insight.** Collage provides extensive views into exactly what is going on with your content so that if you need to audit your content, you have the data at your fingertips.

- **Predictability.** Collage makes content management predictable through easy-to-use processes, automated deployment, and sophisticated user management.
- **Excellent price.** Collage licenses cost significantly less (½ to ⅓) than comparable solutions.
- **Up and running in a few days.** Collage can be installed and configured in a matter of days, not months (or years).
- **Complete and ready to roll.** Collage is designed as packaged software. It isn't a toolkit that requires a lot of development work before you get any value out of it.
- **Familiar look and feel.** Collage acts and behaves like common desktop applications. For example, in Collage's browser-based WYSIWYG editor, if you want to bold a word you can click on the B icon or simply press Ctrl+B, just like you would when working in Microsoft Word. It's nice not to have to fumble for unfamiliar commands!
- **Accessible service.** Collage AnswerLine customer support has won the Omega Management Group's NorthFace award for exemplary service the last three years in a row.

Will Collage Work in My Environment?

Collage is designed to help make your existing infrastructure work better, not to replace it. Collage works with a vast array of leading platforms and technologies available today, including Windows, Solaris, Linux, AIX, Sybase, Oracle, MS SQL, Tomcat, IBM WebSphere, BEA WebLogic, SAP NetWeaver, Oracle Application Server, IIS, Apache, ASP, JSP, PHP, Cold Fusion, .NET, and a whole lot more.

Where to Go for More Information

Seeing the concepts in the context of your own Web site usually helps. If you have an hour and are interested in getting a demo of how content management software can help solve your Web content challenges, submit a request at `www.serena.com/showme`. A Serena representative will gladly show you just how simple taking control of your existing Web sites can be.

About Serena

Serena Software, Inc. (Nasdaq: SRNA) is the world's largest company solely focused on managing change throughout the application lifecycle. Serena serves the complex change-management needs of 49 of the Fortune 50, and its products are in use at over 16,000 customer sites worldwide.